Scholastic Success With
Vocabulary

Grade 2

by Danette Randolph

New York • Toronto • London • Auckland • Sydney
Mexico City • New Delhi • Hong Kong • Buenos Aires

Teaching *Resources*

Cover art by Amy Vangsgard
Cover design by Maria Lilja
Interior illustrations by Sherry Neidigh
Interior design by Quack & Company

ISBN 0-439-55381-4

11 12   40   09

Introduction

Developing a rich vocabulary is an important key to learning. Students who have a wide vocabulary and become independent word learners score higher on achievement tests and are both successful in school and beyond. Parents and teachers alike will find this book a valuable teaching tool in helping students become independent word learners. Students will enjoy completing the activities as they encounter a vast and varied vocabulary including rhyming words, synonyms, antonyms, short vowel sounds, and much more. The activities are both engaging and educational. Take a look at the Table of Contents and you will feel rewarded knowing you're providing such a valuable resource for your students. Remember to praise them for their efforts and successes.

Table of Contents

Day by Day (Days of the week) 4

Let's Celebrate! (Months/holidays) 5

Just the Right Spot (Rhyming words) 6

Dynamically Different (Antonyms) 7

Strikingly Similar (Synonyms) 8

Some Similar Sounds (Homophones) 9

Side by Side (Compound words) 10

Quacking Fun (Sound-effect words) 11

Which Star? (Homonyms) 12

There's Nothing Like a Book!
    (Elements of a story) 13

Search for Clues (Using context clues) 14

All Shipshape (Geometry vocabulary) 15

Math Words (Math vocabulary) 16

Wonderful Weather (Weather vocabulary) . . .17

Interesting Insect Facts (Insects) 18

Friends of Long Ago (Dinosaurs) 19

A Flower's Job (Flowers) 20

Neighbors in Space (Planets) 21

Career Choices (Careers) 22

Time to Travel (Transportation) 23

Many Maps (Maps) 24

All Around Town (Maps) 25

All Across America (Landmarks) 26

Home for One and All (Geography) 27

Home Sweet Home (Animal habitats) 28

It All Adds Up! (Economics) 29

How Are You Feeling? (Emotions) 30

Character Caps (Character traits) 31

Wagon Wheel (Short-a sound) 32

A Pig in a Pen (Short-e sound) 33

Get a Hit! (Short-i sound) 34

Let's Play Hockey! (Short-o sound) 35

Oh! A Smudge! (Short-u sound) 36

Planting a Garden (Long vowel sounds) 37

Moving Up (Nouns) 38

Making Matches (Proper nouns) 39

Details, Details (Adjectives) 40

Time for Action (Verbs) 41

Adding Up Adverbs (Adverbs) 42

Short and Simple (Contractions) 43

Let It Snow! (Analogies) 44

Give It Your Best Swing! (Analogies) 45

Apple Picking (Analogies) 46

Answer Key 47

Day by Day

Write the correct day in each empty balloon.

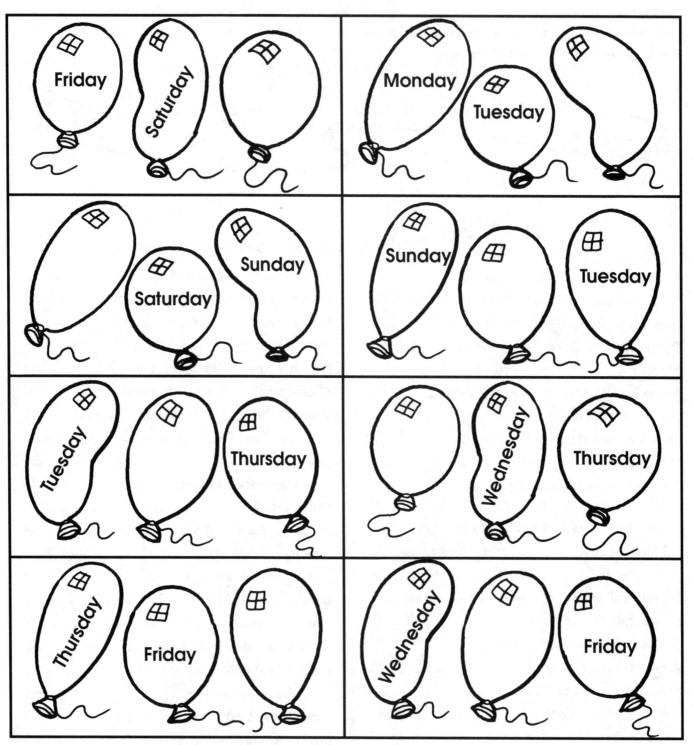

How many days are in a week? _____ How many weeks are in a month? _____
How many months are in a year? _____

Let's Celebrate!

Use the grid to write the month for each holiday. Color your three favorite holidays.

4	April	December	May
3	October	February	August
2	January	June	March
1	July	November	September
	A	**B**	**C**

Flag Day	Earth Day	Halloween	Martin Luther King, Jr. Day
_____ (B, 2)	_____ (A, 4)	_____ (A, 3)	_____ (A, 2)
Christmas	**St. Patrick's Day**	**Presidents' Day**	**Columbus Day**
_____ (B, 4)	_____ (C, 2)	_____ (B, 3)	_____ (A, 3)
New Year's Day	**Memorial Day**	**Valentine's Day**	**Thanksgiving**
_____ (A, 2)	_____ (C, 4)	_____ (B, 3)	_____ (B, 1)
Kwanzaa	**Independence Day**	**Labor Day**	**Hanukkah**
_____ (B, 4)	_____ (A, 1)	_____ (C, 1)	_____ (B, 4)

Just the Right Spot

The rows in each parking lot contain words that rhyme, going across.
Write the words in the empty spaces to show where the incoming cars
should park.

| bead | | |

| let | |

| shake |

seed	knead	
	bake	rake
wet		fret

there		hair
ground		sound
tramp		lamp

| wear | camp |
| found | |

would		could
	date	skate
	flush	slush

| brush | |
| ate |
| should |

 On another sheet of paper, create another rhyming grid. Use the words *sky*, *hop*, **and** *sing*.

Scholastic Teaching Resources

Dynamically Different

Antonyms *are words with opposite meanings.*

Write an antonym for each clue
to complete the crossword puzzle.
Use the words in the Word Bank
below to help you.

Across	Down
1. smile	**2.** new
4. right	**3.** south
6. clean	**4.** big
9. sad	**5.** last
11. start	**7.** close
12. wide	**8.** lost
14. rough	**10.** down
16. under	**13.** forget
	15. short

Word Bank

tall	over	smooth
left	dirty	across
first	north	happy
old	open	remember
stop	frown	narrow
little	found	

On another sheet of paper, draw a picture to show
the antonyms *right* and *left*.

Strikingly Similar

A **synonym** is a word that means the same or nearly the same as another word.

Circle every other letter. Write the circled letters in order on the line to name the synonym for each word. The first one has been done for you.

begin	s (s) y (t) n (a) o (r) n (t)	_____ start
glad	y h m a s p a p r y	_____
tell	e s w a o y	_____
loud	r n d o s i t s h y	_____
little	a s t m h a a l v l	_____
look	e p t e h e e k	_____
large	s b a i m g	_____
fearful	e a m f e r a a n i i d	_____
group	n s g e s t	_____

Write the letters you did not circle in order on the blanks to complete the sentence.

_ _ _ _ _ _ _ _ _   _ _ _   _ _ _ _   _ _ _ _

_ _ _ _   _ _ _   _ _ _ _ _   _ _ _ _ _ _ _ _ .

Some Similar Sounds

Homophones *are words that sound alike but have different spellings and different meanings.*

Add or subtract letters to spell the homophone of the first word. Write the homophone that fits the sentence. The first one has been done for you.

1. deer – er + ar = ___dear___   The ___deer___ jumped the fence to safety.

2. two – w = _____   A duet is made of _____ singers.

3. sun – u + o = _____   The father took his _____ to the game.

4. scent – s = _____   The _____ of flowers filled the room.

5. chili – i + ly = _____   Wear a coat when it is _____.

6. their – ir + re = _____   Your books are _____ on the table.

7. know – k – w = _____   The sign says _____ swimming.

8. hair – ir + re = _____   Brush your _____ before school.

9. wee – e = _____   He was a _____ little lad.

10. here – re + ar = _____   Listen closely to _____ the directions.

11. weight – eight + ait = _____   The rock's _____ was great.

12. break – eak + ake = _____   It is time for a _____.

On another sheet of paper, write two sentences with homophones not used in the sentences above.

Side by Side

 A **compound word** *is a word made by joining two words together to make a new word.*

Complete the crossword puzzle with the missing part of each compound word. Use the Word Bank to help you.

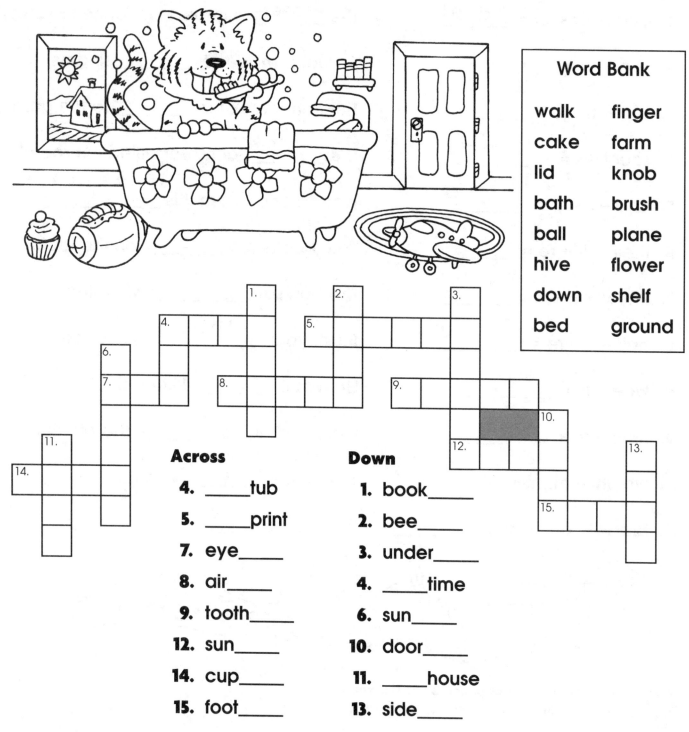

Word Bank

walk	finger
cake	farm
lid	knob
bath	brush
ball	plane
hive	flower
down	shelf
bed	ground

Across

4. _____tub
5. _____print
7. eye_____
8. air_____
9. tooth_____
12. sun_____
14. cup_____
15. foot_____

Down

1. book_____
2. bee_____
3. under_____
4. _____time
6. sun_____
10. door_____
11. _____house
13. side_____

Name _____

Quacking Fun

➡ *Some words let a reader "hear" what is happening. For example: munch and quack*

Write the word from the box that sounds like what is happening in each picture. Then use the code to answer the riddle below.

croak	slam	growl	squeak	crack
snap	fizz	thud	roar	buzz

1.

2.

3.

4.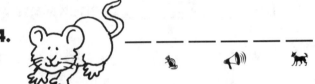

5.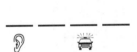

6.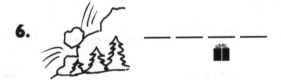

7.

8.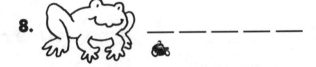

9.

10.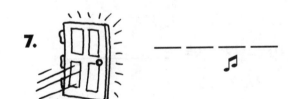

What do you call a bunch of ducks in a box?

Name _____

Which Star?

 Homonyms *are words that have more than one meaning.* .

Write the word from a star that can be used in both blanks in each sentence. The first one has been done for you.

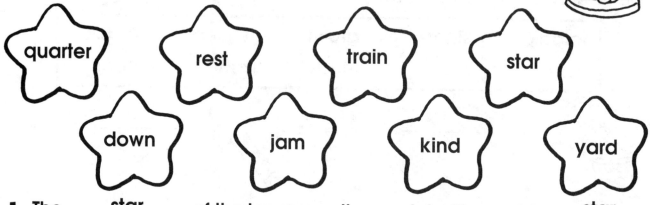

quarter   rest   train   star

down   jam   kind   yard

1. The _____star_____ of the team won the medal with a gold ___star___.

2. It was a _____ to five when I spent my last _____.

3. We found a _____ of ribbon while playing in the _____.

4. Juan threw the _____ pillow _____ from the top bunk.

5. Amber wanted to _____ before finishing the _____ of her homework.

6. The _____ woman let me choose my favorite _____ of ice cream.

7. Christy needs to _____ her dog before they ride on the _____.

8. Scott ate toast and _____ during the traffic _____.

 On another sheet of paper, write a sentence that shows both meanings of the words *spring,* *orange,* **and** *light.*

There's Nothing Like a Book!

Use the grid to complete each sentence.

1. The middle of the story usually has a problem called the _____.
   (A, 1)

2. Stories written in rhyme are called _____.
   (B, 1)

3. The _____ tells where the story takes place.
   (B, 2)

4. The _____ writes the story.
   (A, 3)

5. Each story has a name or _____.
   (B, 5)

6. The _____ draws pictures to go with the story.
   (B, 6)

7. Some stories are make-believe or _____.
   (A, 2)

8. People in the story are called _____.
   (A, 4)

9. The _____ happens near the end of the story and fixes the problem.
   (A, 6)

10. The _____ of a story is the lesson it teaches to the reader.
    (B, 3)

11. A story that really could happen is _____.
    (A, 5)

12. Stories and poems are both kinds of _____.
    (B, 4)

GRID

	A	B
6	solution	illustrator
5	realistic	title
4	characters	literature
3	author	moral
2	fantasy	setting
1	conflict	poetry

Name _____

Using context clues

Search for Clues

➡ *One way to find out the meaning of a new word in a sentence is to use all the other words to figure out what makes sense. This is called using **context clues**.*

Use the meaning of the words in each sentence to choose the missing word from the Word Bank. Write the word in the boxes. Then write the letters from the shaded boxes in order on the line below to answer the question.

Word Bank

agree	value	burst
gain	graph	duty
cure	split	elect

1. Take this medicine to ☐☐☐☐ your cough.

2. The ☐☐☐☐☐ of a quarter is 25 cents.

3. Nick wants to ☐☐☐☐ 10 pounds this year.

4. We must ☐☐☐☐☐ on a place to meet.

5. The team voted to ☐☐☐☐☐ a captain.

6. It is Mara's ☐☐☐☐ to clean the table after lunch.

7. Let's ☐☐☐☐☐ the candy bar into two pieces.

8. The balloon will ☐☐☐☐☐ if you stick a pin in it.

9. The ☐☐☐☐☐ shows how many books each student read.

What language has the most words? _____

14   Scholastic Success With Vocabulary • Grade 2

Scholastic Teaching Resources

Name _____

Geometry vocabulary

All Shipshape

Unscramble each geometry word and write it on the line. Use the words in the box to help you. Then color the box and the matching shape the color listed below the line.

circle	rectangle	cylinder	cube	oval
square	triangle	cone	diamond	hexagon

suqera	_____ red
tigaelrn	_____ white
anreclget	_____ black
neco	_____ blue
addmoin	_____ green
becu	_____ pink
xhanoge	_____ purple
lvoa	_____ yellow
lyncdrie	_____ orange
rcclie	_____ brown

Scholastic Teaching Resources

Scholastic Success With Vocabulary • Grade 2   15

Math Words

Use the chart to write the missing words.

g	h	v	y	l	n	q	o	e	i	c	t	m	f	u	r	b	s	d	a	w
1	2	3	4	5	6	7	8	9	10	11	12	13	14	15	16	17	18	19	20	21

1. When you ___ ___ ___ numbers, the answer is the ___ ___ ___ .
      20 19 19   18 15 13

2. When you ___ ___ ___ ___ ___ ___ ___ ___ numbers, the answer
      18 15 17 12 16 20 11 12

is the ___ ___ ___ ___ ___ ___ ___ ___ ___ ___ .
    19 10 14 14 9 16 9 6 11 9

3. The words ___ ___ ___ ___ ___ ___ ___ ___ ___ ___ and
      20 5 12 8 1 9 12 2 9 16

___ ___ ___ ___ ___ in a word problem tell you to add.
 12 8 12 20 5

4. The words ___ ___ ___ ___   ___ ___ ___ ___ and
      2 20 3 9   5 9 14 12

___ ___ ___   ___ ___ ___ ___   ___ ___ ___ ___ in a word
 2 8 21   13 20 6 4   13 8 16 9

problem tell you to subtract.

5. Two numbers of the same value are ___ ___ ___ ___ ___ .
                 9 7 15 20 5

6. When you ___ ___ ___ ___ ___ a problem, you get the answer.
      18 8 5 3 9

List five jobs where math skills are used.

Scholastic Teaching Resources

Wonderful Weather

Add or subtract from each letter to spell different weather words. The first one has been done for you.

a	b	c	d	e	f	g	h	i	j	k	l	m	n	o	p	q	r	s	t	u	v	w	x	y	z

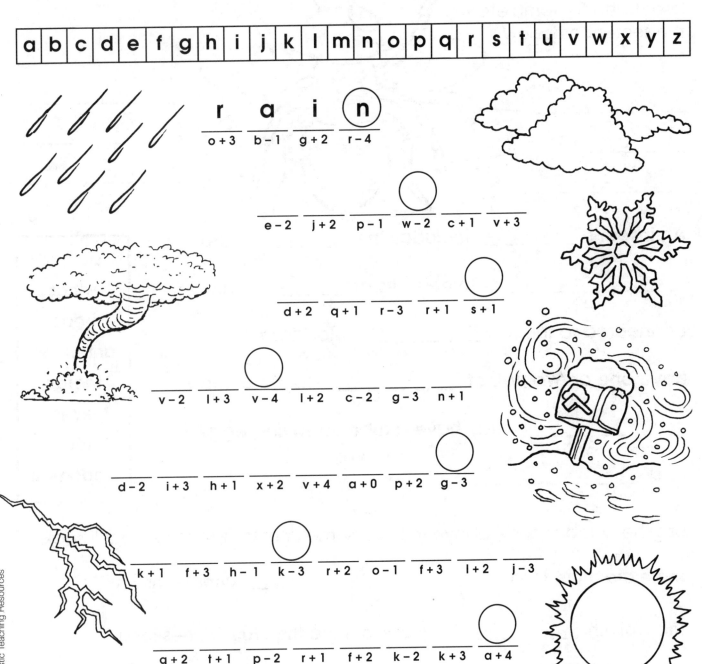

r a i n
o+3 b-1 g+2 r-4

___ ___ ___ (○) ___ ___
e-2 j+2 p-1 w-2 c+1 v+3

___ ___ ___ ___ (○)
d+2 q+1 r-3 r+1 s+1

___ ___ (○) ___ ___ ___ ___
v-2 l+3 v-4 l+2 c-2 g-3 n+1

___ ___ ___ ___ ___ ___ (○)
d-2 i+3 h+1 x+2 v+4 a+0 p+2 g-3

___ ___ ___ (○) ___ ___ ___ ___ ___
k+1 f+3 h-1 k-3 r+2 o-1 f+3 l+2 j-3

___ ___ ___ ___ ___ ___ ___ (○)
q+2 t+1 p-2 r+1 f+2 k-2 k+3 a+4

Unscramble the circled letters to spell weather you hear but cannot see. ___ ___ ___ ___ ___ ___ ___

Interesting Insect Facts

Use the words in the box
to label each part of an
insect and to complete
the sentences below.

_____

_____

_____

_____

_____

_____

_____

_____

An insect's _ _ _ _ includes the _ _ _ _ and
        3   9

_ _ _ _ _ _ _ _. Three pairs of _ _ _ _ are
10   2   6

connected to the _ _ _ _ _ _. Most insects
                  8   1

have one or two pair of _ _ _ _ _. The tip of the

_ _ _ _ _ _ _ may have a tube for laying eggs
7   4

or a _ _ _ _ _ _ _.
     5

| stinger |
| wings |
| head |
| antennae |
| thorax |
| eyes |
| legs |
| abdomen |

Use the number code above to learn some interesting facts about insects.

There are more than _ _ _   _ _ _ _ _ _ kinds of insects.
                     1 2 3. 4 5 6 6 5 1 2

The Goliath _ _ _ _ _ _ grows to more than four inches long.
            7 3 3 8 6 3

An _ _ _ _ _ moth is about 1,000 times larger than a tiny fairy fly.
   10 8 6 10 9

On another sheet of paper, draw an imaginary insect. Label the body parts. Be sure to
give the insect a name.

Scholastic Teaching Resources

Friends of Long Ago

A paleontologist is a person who studies dinosaurs. Several dinosaurs that paleontologists have studied are listed below. Use the letters in *paleontologist* to write the names of these dinosaurs below their meanings.

1. "Winged and Toothless" p _ _ _ a _ _ _ _	**2.** "Double Beamed" _ _ _ _ l _ _ _ _ _
3. "Great Lizard" _ e _ _ _ o _ _ _ _	**4.** "Iguana Tooth" _ _ _ _ n _ _ _ _
5. "Deceptive Lizard" _ _ _ t _ o _ _ _ _ _ _	**6.** "Speedy Thief" _ _ l o _ _ _ _ _ _ _
7. "Roofed Lizard" _ _ _ g _ _ _ _ _ _	**8.** "Arm Lizard" _ _ _ _ _ i _ _ _ _ _ _
9. "Different Lizard" _ _ _ _ _ s _ _ _ _	**10.** "Three-Horned Face" t _ _ _ _ _ _ _ _ _

velociraptor   allosaurus   stegosaurus   iguanodon

brachiosaurus   triceratops   pteranodon   megalosaurus

diplodocus   apatosaurus

Research one of the dinosaurs above. On another sheet of paper, write five words that describe this dinosaur.

A Flower's Job

Use the words in the box to label each part of the flower and to complete the sentences below.

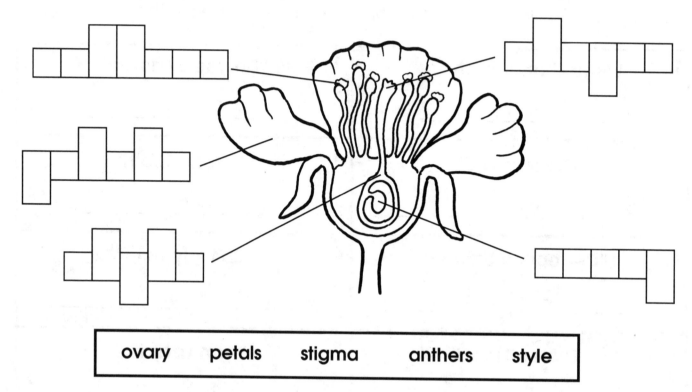

| ovary | petals | stigma | anthers | style |

A flower is important in the life cycle of a plant because it contains the parts for reproduction. The colorful _ _ t _ _ _ and sepals protect the flower when it is in bud. The sticky part in the middle of the flower is the _ _ _ g _ _ . Around the stigma are _ n _ _ _ _ _ which are tiny stems with knobs on top. Inside the anthers is a golden dust called pollen. In the base of the flower is the _ v _ _ _ . Growing out of the ovary is the _ _ y _ _ . When ripe, the anthers burst open sending out clouds of pollen. The pollen is carried to the stigma of another flower. This is called pollination.

Scholastic Teaching Resources

Neighbors in Space

Read each clue. Write the name to label each planet.

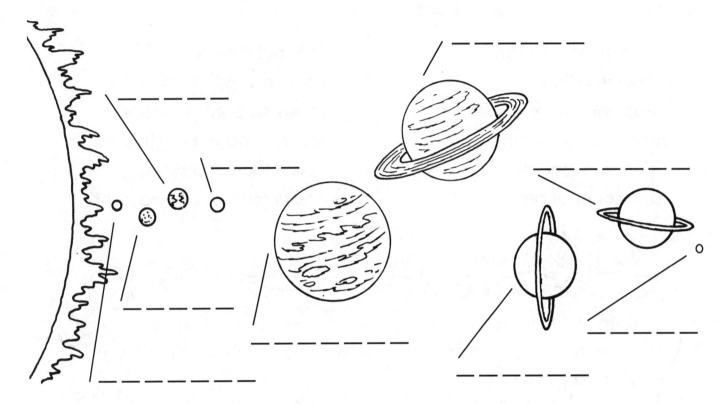

Pluto is the smallest planet.

Jupiter is the largest planet and is made mostly of gas. It has a spot called the Great Red Spot.

Neptune is the second to last planet from the sun.

Saturn is made of gas with bright rings around it.

Earth, the third planet from the sun, is the only planet with oceans of water.

Mercury is a very hot planet because it is closest to the sun.

Venus passes nearer to Earth than any other planet.

Uranus is the seventh planet from the sun. It is the only one tipped on its side.

Mars is the fourth planet from the sun. Its rustlike color comes from the large amount of iron in its soil.

 Color the planet you live on green and blue.

Career Choices

Use the clues below to circle the names of different careers in the puzzle. The names go across and down.

helps students learn	puts out fires
works in a library	delivers mail
keeps neighborhoods safe	drives students to school
takes care of teeth	serves food at a restaurant
treats sick people	sells things at a store
takes care of pets	cooks food at a restaurant

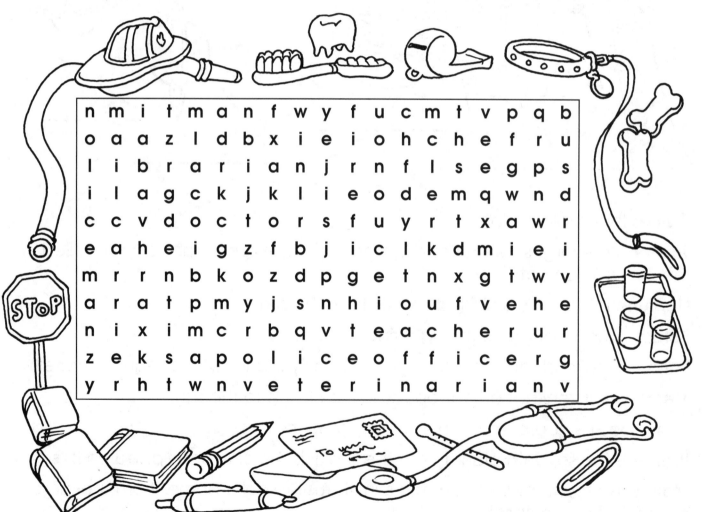

```
n m i t m a n f w y f u c m t v p q b
o a a z l d b x i e i o h c h e f r u
l i b r a r i a n j r n f l s e g p s
i l a g c k j k l i e o d e m q w n d
c c v d o c t o r s f u y r t x a w r
e a h e i g z f b j i c l k d m i e i
m r r n b k o z d p g e t n x g t w v
a r a t p m y j s n h i o u f v e h e
n i x i m c r b q v t e a c h e r u r
z e k s a p o l i c e o f f i c e r g
y r h t w n v e t e r i n a r i a n v
```

 On another sheet of paper, write about what you want to be when you grow up. Give three reasons why.

Time to Travel

Unscramble each transportation word. Then color the boxes according to the chart.

red = land	
purple = air	
yellow = water	

	orcleymtco	
	_____	
palniera	**ritna**	**ltechopire**
_____	_____	_____
hpsi	**sbu**	**msbunirae**
_____	_____	_____
slotabia	**uktcr**	**refyr**
_____	_____	_____
asecp hutltes	**rca**	**tje**
_____	_____	_____
	vna	
	_____	

 On another sheet of paper, write a story about taking a trip to the moon.

Many Maps

Use the code to identify each map.

h	f	p	m	a	r	o	b	g	l	t	d	n	e	w	u	i
1	2	3	4	5	6	7	8	9	10	11	12	13	14	15	16	17

A __ __ __ __ map shows the best way to get somewhere.
   6 7 5 12

A __ __ __ __ __ __ __ map shows the weather of a certain area.
  15 14 5 11 1 14 6

A __ __ __ __ __ __ map shows how high and low the land is in an area.
  6 14 10 17 14 2

A __ __ __ __ __ __ __ __ __ __ map shows the number of people in an area.
  3 7 3 16 10 5 11 17 7 13

A __ __ __ __ __ __ __ __ map shows the shape and features of an area.
  10 5 13 12 2 7 6 4

A __ __ __ __ __ is a round model of Earth.
  9 10 7 8 14

Label the kinds of maps shown below.

_____   _____   _____

Which map would you use to select a warm place to visit for vacation?

Scholastic Teaching Resources

Name _____

All Around Town

Use the Map Key to read the map. Complete each sentence below.

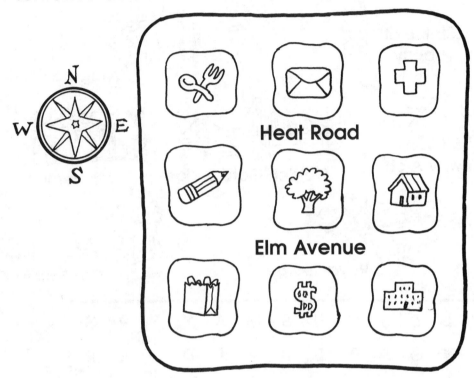

Heat Road

Elm Avenue

1. The ⬜🔲⬜⬜⬜⬜ is north of the grocery store.

2. The post office is east of the ⬜⬜⬜🔲⬜🔲⬜🔲

3. There are ⬜🔲⬜⬜ south of the hospital.

4. The 🔲⬜⬜⬜⬜⬜⬜ ⬜⬜🔲⬜ is west of the bank.

5. There are 🔲⬜⬜⬜⬜⬜⬜⬜ south of the houses.

6. You must cross 🔲🔲⬜⬜ 🔲⬜⬜⬜ to go from the post office to the park.

Write the letters from the shaded boxes in order on the line to learn a new word.

A mapmaker is called a _____.

All Across America

Circle the name of each American landmark shown. The names go across, down, and diagonally.

Mt. Rushmore

Statue of Liberty

Niagara Falls

Plymouth Rock

Gateway Arch

Golden Gate Bridge

Mt. Vernon

Grand Canyon

Royal Gorge

Old Faithful

```
M T P F A L L S R U S M A Y F R G
G O L D E N G A T E B R I D G E R
N J Y M T R U S H M O R E S O N A
I G M G S E O E L A R O C K L E N
A R O J A N E Y C A N G R A D W D
G D U U M T F I A R S T B R I D C
A S T A T U E O F L I B E R T Y A
R S H Y V G A W T E G O L D L A N
A T R O E R O Y A A T O A R C F Y
F U O N R U S H E Y O F R F U L O
A L C I N E W R U S A B E G R T N
L Y K M O R E G R A N R D C E A N
L O N G N A T B R I P L C Y M O U
S P I N N S O L D F A I T H F U L
```

Home for One and All

Use the code to complete the sentences below. Then write the number of each place in the correct circle on the map.

e	o	f	a	n	s	u	r	l	m	d	h	c	t	p	i	g
1	2	3	4	5	6	7	8	9	10	11	12	13	14	15	16	17

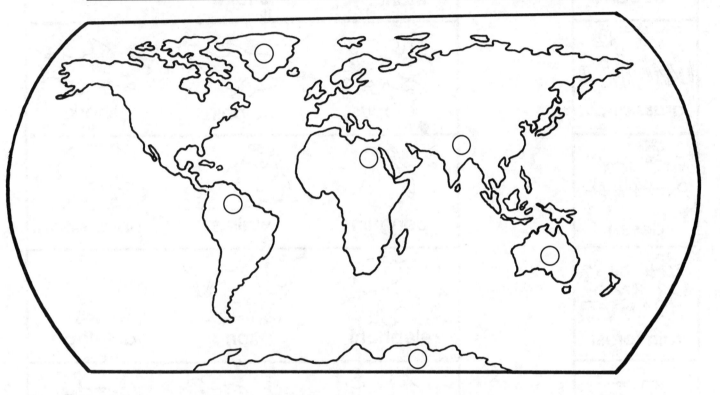

1. The smallest continent on Earth is __ __ __ __ __ __ __ __ __.
4   7   6   14   8   4   9   16   4

2. The highest mountain on Earth is Mt. Everest in __ __ __ __.
4   6   16   4

3. The largest island on Earth is __ __ __ __ __ __ __ __ __.
17   8   1   1   5   9   4   5   11

4. The longest river on Earth is the Nile on the continent of
__ __ __ __ __ __.
4   3   8   16   13   4

5. The highest waterfall on Earth is in
__ __ __ __ __   __ __ __ __ __ __ __.
6   2   7   14   12   4   10   1   8   16   13   4

6. The coldest place on Earth is __ __ __ __ __ __ __ __ __ __.
4   5   14   4   8   13   14   16   13   4

Home Sweet Home

Draw a line to match each habitat to the animals that live there.

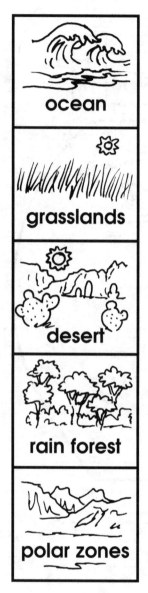

ocean

grasslands

desert

rain forest

polar zones

monkey
1

snake
10

ape

octopus
6

dolphin

shark
5

penguin
7

walrus
9

polar bear
3

elephant
2

lion

antelope
11

camel
4

lizard

coyote
8

Use the numbered letters above to complete the animal facts.

The world's largest animal is the __ __ __ __   __ __ __ __ __ __.
3 4 7 1   9 2 5 4 1

One of the world's slowest animals is the __ __ __ __ __.
10 4 8 11 2

One of the world's fastest animals is the __ __ __ __ __ __ __.
6 2 1 1 11 5 2

It All Adds Up!

Solve each addition and subtraction problem. Use the answers to match each word to its definition.

consumer	22¢ + 15¢	97¢ − 76¢	coin or paper money
want	20¢ + 20¢	59¢ − 22¢	someone who buys or uses things
need	37¢ + 10¢	78¢ − 22¢	a person who makes a product or provides a service
currency	11¢ + 10¢	98¢ − 58¢	something we would like to have, above our needs
producer	32¢ + 24¢	80¢ − 30¢	place for depositing and borrowing money
product	7¢ + 2¢	49¢ − 40¢	something made or grown
service	11¢ + 20¢	88¢ − 41¢	something we must have for survival
labor	20¢ + 10¢	60¢ − 30¢	work
bank	20¢ + 30¢	99¢ − 68¢	a helpful act or job

How Are You Feeling?

Read the message in each bubble. Choose a feeling word from the box below that goes with the message. Write it on the blanks. Then draw a face to match that feeling.

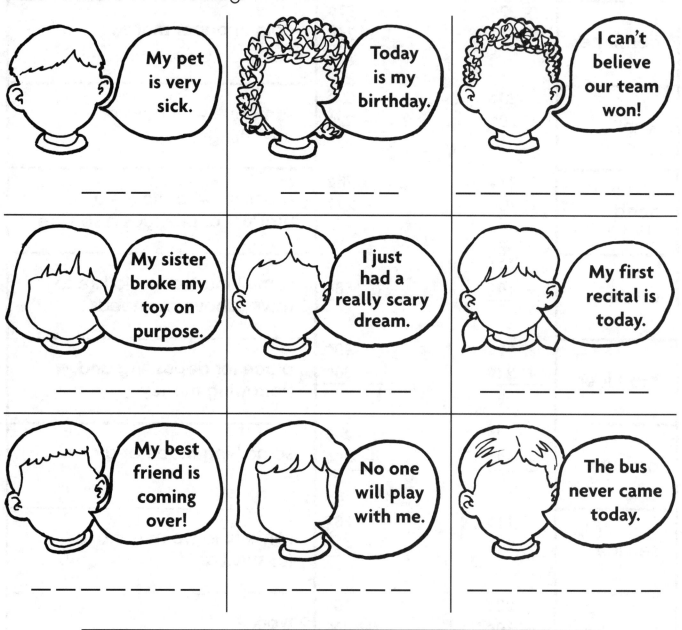

My pet is very sick.	Today is my birthday.	I can't believe our team won!
_ _ _ _ _	_ _ _ _ _	_ _ _ _ _ _ _
My sister broke my toy on purpose.	I just had a really scary dream.	My first recital is today.
_ _ _ _ _	_ _ _ _ _	_ _ _ _ _ _ _
My best friend is coming over!	No one will play with me.	The bus never came today.
_ _ _ _ _	_ _ _ _ _	_ _ _ _ _ _ _

lonely	sad	surprised	angry	nervous
confused	afraid	happy	excited	

 On another sheet of paper, write a thank-you note to a friend who helped you when you were sad.

Scholastic Teaching Resources

Character Caps

Write the character trait described in each sentence. Use the words on the caps as clues. Then use the number code to complete the sentence below.

1.

I finished my homework before going out to play.

___ ___ ___ ___ ___ ___ ___
4   7

2.

I accidentally took my friend's dollar, but I gave it back.

___ ___ ___ ___ ___ ___ ___
2

3.

I worked with all my neighbors and cleaned the street.

___ ___ ___ ___ ___ ___ ___ ___ ___ ___ ___
9 3

4.

I asked the new boy to play with me at recess.

___ ___ ___ ___ ___ ___ ___ ___ ___ ___ ___ ___ ___
6   5

5.

At lunchtime I was very hungry, but I waited my turn in line.

___ ___ ___ ___ ___ ___ ___ ___
8 1

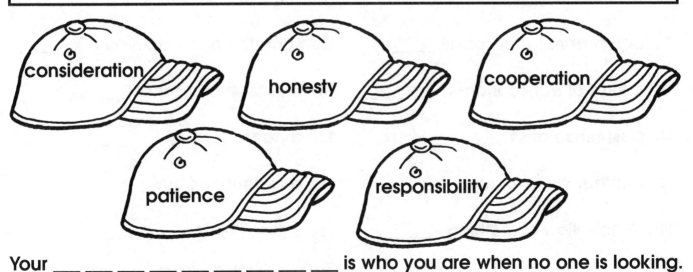

consideration

honesty

cooperation

patience

responsibility

Your ___ ___ ___ ___ ___ ___ ___ ___ ___ is who you are when no one is looking.
    1   2   3   4   5   6   7   8   9

Wagon Wheel

Begin in a small circle. Follow the line to the center circle and then back to another small circle. See how many words with the short-*a* sound you can make. Then write a word with a short-*a* sound for each clue below.

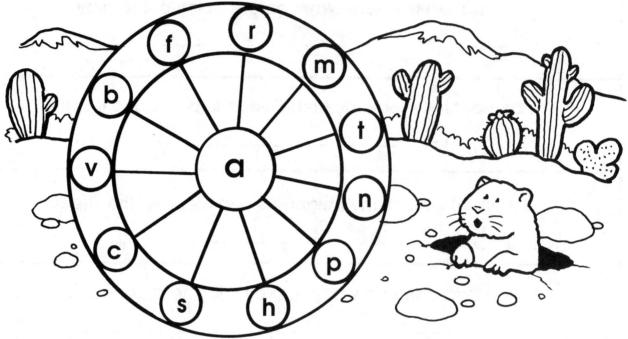

1. a feline friend _____

2. something for your head _____

3. a grown boy _____

4. a name for a boy _____

5. a skin color _____

6. a meat you can eat _____

7. equipment for baseball _____

8. something to cool you off _____

9. a kind of transportation _____

10. opposite of cannot _____

11. past tense of sit _____

12. a name for a girl _____

13. another word for rug _____

14. past tense of run _____

15. to not allow something _____

16. a small rodent _____

 On another sheet of paper, see how many short-a words you can create from the letters in *atmosphere*.

A Pig in a Pen

Begin in any space on the top line. Move down or diagonally to end on the bottom line and spell a word with a short-e sound. Write each word in the boxes. The first one has been done for you.

w	l	v	s	b	n	h	m	d	p
a	e	f	e	u	e	a	e	c	e
b	t	e	t	d	b	t	o	n	t

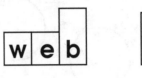 w e b

Use a word with a short-e sound from above to complete each sentence.

A home for a spider is a _____.

A home for a pillow is a _____.

A home for a fox is a _____.

A home for a pig is a _____.

A home for a sick animal is with a _____.

A home for a duck is a place that is _____.

 On another sheet of paper, see how many short-e words you can create from the letters in *elephant*.

Get a Hit!

Write a word with the short-*i* sound that goes with each clue in the matching circle. Change one letter of the last word as you work around the baseball diamond.

1. a lie

2. to correct a mistake

3. to stir things together

4. one more than five

5. something you do on a chair

6. a candle with a flame

7. a good sense of humor

8. to be the first one to finish a race

9. part of a fish   10. clothes that are the right size

11. a popular song   12. a pronoun for a boy

13. a room with little light   14. chips and ____

15. something left for a waiter

16. one small drink   17. top of your leg

18. part of your mouth

19. top of a jar

20. to make an offer

Let's Play Hockey!

Use the words on the hockey pucks to finish each sentence with a word with the short-*o* sound. Then use the letters in the special shapes to finish the sentence below.

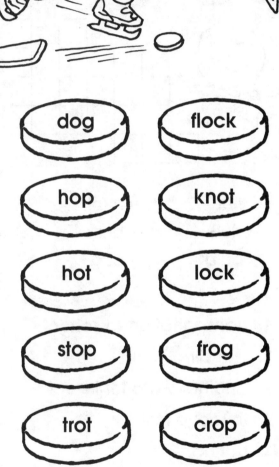

1. ___o____ the door.

2. Tie it in a _____.

3. Horses sometimes ___ ___o___.

4. A farmer plants a ___ ___o___.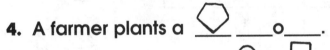

5. The summer sun feels ___o___.

6. A ___ ___o___ sits on a lily pad.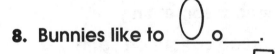

7. A bone is a treat for a ___o___.

8. Bunnies like to ___o___.

9. A red light means ___ ___o___.

10. Sheep travel in a ___ ___o___.

Hockey pucks:
- dog
- flock
- hop
- knot
- hot
- lock
- stop
- frog
- trot
- crop

___o___ey wa___ i___ve___e___ i___ ___a___a___ a.

 On another sheet of paper, see how many short-*o* words you can create from the letters in *octopus*.

Oh! A Smudge!

Complete the crossword puzzle with words that have the short-*u* sound.
Use the Word Bank to help you.

Word Bank

nut	mutt	scrub	grudge	run
dull	bus	smudge	mud	sun
bulb	bug	bubble	tub	drug

Across

1. transportation to school
5. wet dirt
8. another word for insect
9. to move fast
12. boring
13. stay mad at someone, holding a ____
14. a kind of gum
15. something buried by a squirrel

Down

2. to smear something
3. a source of light on Earth
4. to really wash something
6. a medicine
7. a light____
10. a mixed breed of dog
11. a place for a bath

 On another sheet of paper, see how many short-u words you can create from the letters in *unquestionable*.

Name _____

Planting a Garden

Use the grid to write the missing words in the story.

4	came	raked	grow	faces	row	Kate
3	placed	brightly	hole	day	shined	seed
2	slowly	holes	white	straight	see	hoped
1	they	smile	nine	both	five	rain
	A	B	C	D	E	F

One _____ _____ and Mike decided to plant a
(D, 3) (F, 4)

garden. First, _____ _____ the dirt and dug _____
(A, 1) (B, 4) (E, 1)

_____ in a _____ _____. Next, _____
(B, 2) (D, 2) (E, 4) (A, 1)

_____ a _____ in each _____ and
(A, 3) (F, 3) (C, 3)

_____ covered the _____s with dirt. The _____
(A, 2) (F, 3) (F, 1)

_____. Then the sun _____ _____.
(A, 4) (E, 3) (B, 3)

_____ _____ the _____s would _____.
(A, 1) (F, 2) (F, 3) (C, 4)

A _____ covered _____ of their _____ when
(B, 1) (D, 1) (D, 4)

_____ finally got to _____ _____ _____ flowers.
(A, 1) (E, 2) (E, 1) (C, 2)

 On another sheet of paper, draw a picture of Kate and Mike's garden with the flowers.

Moving Up

 *A **noun** is a naming word. It names a person, place, or thing.*

Begin at the bottom of each ladder. Read each word. Color nouns naming people purple. Color nouns naming places green. Color nouns naming things orange. Complete each pattern with a noun and the correct color.

waiter	zoo	hotel
home	table	sister
friend	mother	nurse
school	school	baseball
brother	hat	beach
store	teacher	librarian
man	ballpark	mom

💡 **On another sheet of paper, make a list of your five favorite people, places, and things.**

Scholastic Teaching Resources

Making Matches

A **proper noun** names a special person, place, or thing. It begins with a capital letter.

Draw a line to connect each proper and common noun. Then write the circled letters in order from top to bottom on the lines below to answer the question.

(W)ashington, D.C.	planet
S(a)muel	continent
Row, Row, Row Your Boat	book
September	(s)tore
Martin Luther King, Jr., Day	(h)oliday
Kr(i)sten	boy
Stuart Little	so(n)g
Sam's Market	(g)irl
Africa	stree(t)
Lindell Avenue	country
Jefferson R(o)ckets	team
Venus	month
E(n)gland	city

Which president is known as "The Father of Our Country"?

_____

Details, Details

 An **adjective** *is a describing word.*

Solve each math problem. Then use the code to write a describing word for each picture.

a.	24	s.	72	c.	35
	+ 33		+ 42		+ 42

i.	60	n.	23	l.	20	o.	42	e.	79	t.	70
	+ 29		+ 52		+ 71		+ 56		+ 20		+ 71

g.	61	r.	47	d.	51	f.	37	y.	45	u.	90
	+ 70		+ 22		+ 95		+ 91		+ 73		+ 17

---

77 98 91 98 69 128 107 91
flower

114 98 107 69
lemon

114 141 69 98 75 131
man

89 75 141 99 69 99 114 141 89 75 131
book

128 57 75 77 118
hat

128 91 107 128 128 118
cloud

131 99 75 141 91 99
lamb

146 99 91 89 77 89 98 107 114
dessert

 On another sheet of paper, write five adjectives to describe your room.

Scholastic Teaching Resources

Time for Action

*A **verb** is a word that shows action.*

Read each word. Color the squares that could show action verbs red.

hop	read	cook	write	throw	walk
think	television	run	jog	car	sing
play	shop	color	fly	whistle	study
swing	eat	robot	beautiful	swim	draw
clean	hang	elephant	window	climb	drive
animal	jump	look	scoot	ride	little
nibble	notebook	lift	knit	doll	pretend
paint	skate	envelope	office	scribble	count
roll	bake	watch	gallop	float	sew

Use the picture to write a verb
you can do with your face.   ___ ___ ___ ___ ___

Adding Up Adverbs

 *An **adverb** is a word that tells how, when, or where an action takes place.*

2	3	4	5	6	7	8	9	10	11	12	13	14	15	16	18	19	20
g	k	t	u	r	q	t	o	c	a	e	s	i	f	y	n	v	l

Add. Use the chart to write letters on the blanks
to spell adverbs.

4 + 3	5 + 0	8 + 6	7 + 3	2 + 1	9 + 11	10 + 6

2 + 0	11 + 1	9 + 9	6 + 2	9 + 11	15 + 1

1 + 9	17 + 3	6 + 6	10 + 9	9 + 3	2 + 4	2 + 18	5 + 11

5 + 2	4 + 1	7 + 7	8 + 4	3 + 1	10 + 10	9 + 7

8 + 2	5 + 6	3 + 2	5 + 3	10 + 4	7 + 2	1 + 4	6 + 7	12 + 8	8 + 8

1 + 1	3 + 3	7 + 4	5 + 5	7 + 5	8 + 7	5 + 0	15 + 5	11 + 9	9 + 7

Complete each sentence with an adverb from above.

1. The ballerina _____ danced to the music.

2. The children crossed the street _____.

3. The cat _____ cleaned her new kittens.

4. The boy read his book _____ at the library.

5. The detective _____ solved the mystery.

6. The quarterback _____ threw the football.

Short and Simple

 A **contraction** is a word made from two words. One or more letters are left out. An **apostrophe** (') is used in place of the missing letters.

Use the chart to write a contraction for each shape problem.

⬠	◯	▢	△	⬡	⬭	▭	△	◯	▱	▱	▱
have	not	would	could	will	I	do	they	you	are	we	she

1. ▱ + ⬠ = _ _ _ ' _

2. ▢ + ◯ = _ _ _ _ _ ' _

3. ◯ + ⬠ = _ _ _ ' _

4. ▭ + ⬠ = _ _ ' _

5. ⬭ + ⬡ = _ ' _ _

6. ⬭ + ▢ = _ ' _

7. ▭ + ◯ = _ _ _ ' _

8. △ + ⬠ = _ _ _ _ _ '

9. ▭ + ▱ = _ _ ' _

10. ▱ + ▢ = _ _ _ _ ' _

11. △ + ⬠ = _ _ _ _ _ ' _

12. △ + ▱ = _ _ _ _ ' _

13. ⬭ + ⬠ = _ ' _ _

14. ⬠ + ◯ = _ _ _ _ '

15. △ + ⬡ = _ _ _ _ ' _

16. ◯ + ▱ = _ _ _ ' _

17. ▱ + ◯ = _ _ _ _ ' _

18. △ + ◯ = _ _ _ _ _ ' _

 On another sheet of paper, write one sentence with two different contractions.

Scholastic Teaching Resources

Let It Snow!

Complete the analogy on each mitten. Use the words on the snowflakes to help you.

1. Kitten is to cat as puppy is to _____.

number

son

2. Drum is to beat as horn is to _____.

flower

dog

3. Milk is to glass as coffee is to _____.

hour

4. Parent is to child as father is to _____.

kick

cup

5. Oak is to tree as rose is to _____.

blow

6. F is to letter as 4 is to _____.

7. Baseball is to hit as football is to _____.

8. Day is to week as minute is to _____.

Scholastic Teaching Resources

Give It Your Best Swing!

Complete the analogy on each bat. Use the words on the caps to help you.

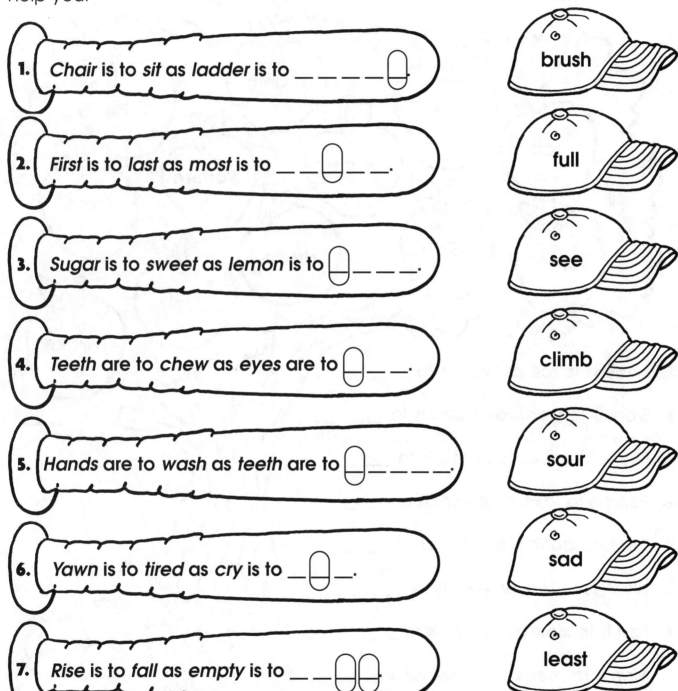

1. *Chair* is to *sit* as *ladder* is to _ _ _ _ _ ⊙ .

2. *First* is to *last* as *most* is to _ _ ⊙ _ _ .

3. *Sugar* is to *sweet* as *lemon* is to ⊙ _ _ _ .

4. *Teeth* are to *chew* as *eyes* are to ⊙ _ _ .

5. *Hands* are to *wash* as *teeth* are to ⊙ _ _ _ _ _ .

6. *Yawn* is to *tired* as *cry* is to _ ⊙ _ .

7. *Rise* is to *fall* as *empty* is to _ _ ⊙ ⊙ _ .

brush

full

see

climb

sour

sad

least

Write the circled letters in the blanks in order to find out what sport was first called "rounders." __ __ __ __ __ __ __

Apple Picking

Complete each analogy with a word on an apple.
Color the apples you used red.

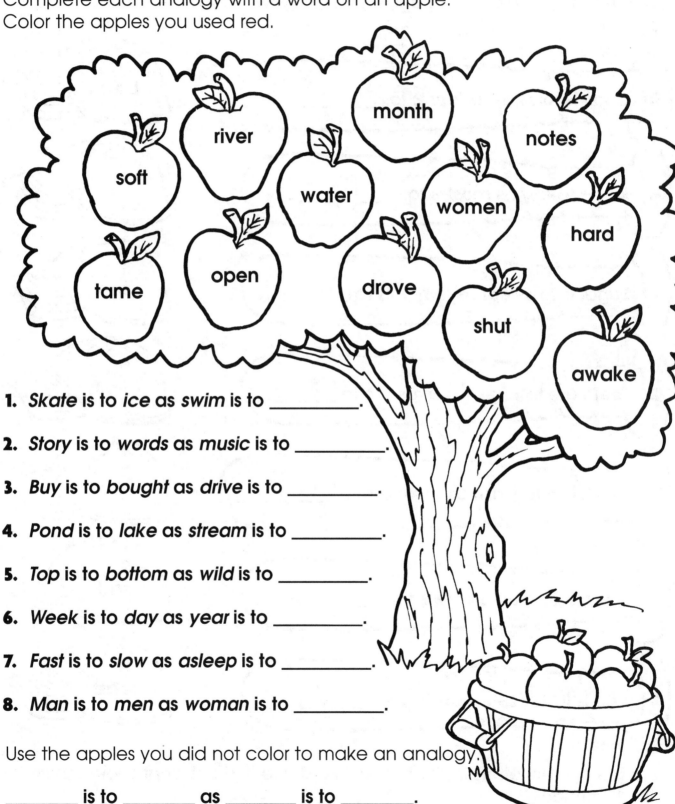

river

soft

month

notes

water

women

hard

tame

open

drove

shut

awake

1. *Skate* is to *ice* as *swim* is to _____.

2. *Story* is to *words* as *music* is to _____.

3. *Buy* is to *bought* as *drive* is to _____.

4. *Pond* is to *lake* as *stream* is to _____.

5. *Top* is to *bottom* as *wild* is to _____.

6. *Week* is to *day* as *year* is to _____.

7. *Fast* is to *slow* as *asleep* is to _____.

8. *Man* is to *men* as *woman* is to _____.

Use the apples you did not color to make an analogy.

_____ is to _____ as _____ is to _____.

Page 4
Sunday, Wednesday;
Friday, Monday;
Wednesday, Tuesday;
Saturday, Thursday

Page 5
June, April, October,
January; December,
March, February, October;
January, May, February,
November; December,
July, September,
December

Page 6

seed	knead	bead
shake	bake	rake
wet	let	fret

there	wear	hair
ground	found	sound
tramp	camp	lamp

would	should	could
ate	date	skate
brush	flush	slush

Page 7

Page 8
happy, say, noisy, small,
peek, big, afraid, set;
Synonyms are words that
have the same meanings.

Page 9
2. to, two; 3. son, son;
4. cent, scent; 5. chilly,
chilly; 6. there, there;
7. no, no; 8. hare, hair;
9. we, wee; 10. hear, hear;
11. wait, weight;
12. brake, break

Page 10

Page 11
1. fizz; 2. crack; 3. snap;
4. squeak; 5. roar; 6. thud;
7. slam; 8. croak; 9. buzz;
10. growl;
a box of quackers!

Page 12
2. quarter; 3. yard;
4. down; 5. rest;
6. kind; 7. train; 8. jam

Page 13
1. conflict; 2. poetry;
3. setting; 4. author;
5. title; 6. illustrator;
7. fantasy; 8. characters;
9. solution; 10. moral;
11. realistic; 12. literature

Page 14
1. cure; 2. value; 3. gain;
4. agree; 5. elect; 6. duty;
7. split; 8. burst; 9. graph;
English

Page 15
square, triangle, rectangle,
cone, diamond, cube,
hexagon, oval, cylinder,
circle

Page 16
1. add, sum; 2. subtract,
difference; 3. altogether,
total; 4. have left, how
many more; 5. equal;
6. solve

Page 17
cloudy, frost, tornado,
blizzard, lightning,
sunshine;
thunder

Page 18
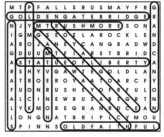

head, eyes, antennae,
legs, thorax, wings,
abdomen, stinger; one
million; beetle; Atlas

Page 19
1. pteranodon;
2. diplodocus;
3. megalosaurus;
4. iguanodon;
5. apatosaurus;
6. velociraptor;
7. stegosaurus;
8. brachiosaurus;
9. allosaurus;
10. triceratops

Page 20
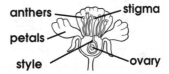

petals, stigma, anthers,
ovary, style

Page 21
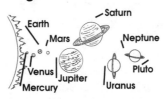

Page 22
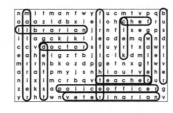

Page 23
motorcycle; airplane, train,
helicopter; ship, bus,
submarine; sailboat, truck,
ferry; space shuttle, car,
jet; van

Page 24
road, weather, relief,
population, landform,
globe;
road map, globe, weather
map

Page 25
1. school; 2. restaurant;
3. houses; 4. grocery store;
5. apartments;
6. Heat Road;
cartographer

Page 26

Page 27
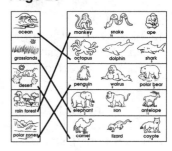

1. Australia; 2. Asia;
3. Greenland; 4. Africa;
5. South America;
6. Antarctica

Page 28
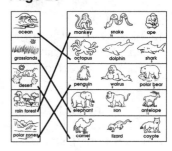

blue whale, sloth, cheetah

Page 29

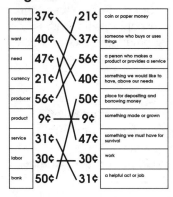

consumer	37¢	21¢	coin or paper money
want	40¢	37¢	someone who buys or uses things
need	47¢	56¢	a person who makes a product or provides a service
currency	21¢	40¢	something we would like to have, above our needs
producer	56¢	50¢	place for depositing and borrowing money
product	9¢	9¢	something made or grown
service	31¢	47¢	something we must have for survival
labor	30¢	30¢	work
bank	50¢	31¢	a helpful act or job

Page 30

sad, happy, surprised; angry, afraid, nervous; excited, lonely, confused

Page 31

1. responsibility;
2. honesty; 3. cooperation;
4. consideration;
5. patience;
character

Page 32

1. cat; 2. hat/cap; 3. man;
4. Sam/Pat; 5. tan; 6. ham;
7. bat; 8. fan; 9. van;
10. can; 11. sat;
12. Pam/Pat/Sam; 13. mat;
14. ran; 15. ban; 16. rat

Page 33

The order may vary: pen; hen, set; wet, let, net, vet, men; den, met, bet, bed, pet;
web, bed, den, pen, vet, wet

Page 34

1. fib; 2. fix; 3. mix; 4. six;
5. sit; 6. lit; 7. wit; 8. win;
9. fin; 10. fit; 11. hit;
12. him; 13. dim; 14. dip;
15. tip; 16. sip; 17. hip;
18. lip; 19. lid; 20. bid

Page 35

1. lock; 2. knot; 3. trot;
4. crop; 5. hot; 6. frog;
7. dog; 8. hop; 9. stop;
10. flock;
Hockey was invented in Canada.

Page 36

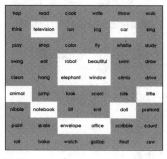

Page 37

day, Kate, they, raked, five, holes, straight, row, they, placed, seed, hole, slowly, seed, rain, came, shined, brightly, They, hoped, seed, grow, smile, both, faces, they, see, five, white

Page 38

Page 39

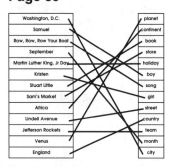

Washington

Page 40

A. 57; S. 114; C. 77; I. 89;
N. 75; L. 91; O. 98; E. 99;
T. 141; G. 131; R. 69;
D. 146; F. 128; Y. 118;
U. 107; colorful, sour;
strong, interesting; fancy, fluffy; gentle, delicious

Page 41

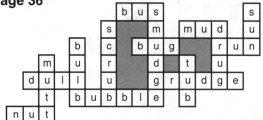

smile

Page 42

quickly, gently, cleverly, quietly, cautiously, gracefully; Answers may vary. Suggested answers include: 1. gracefully;
2. cautiously; 3. gently;
4. quietly; 5. cleverly;
6. quickly

Page 43

1. she'll; 2. wouldn't;
3. you've; 4. we'll;
5. I'll; 6. I'd; 7. don't;
8. they've; 9. we're;
10. she'd; 11. could've;
12. they're; 13. I've;
14. haven't; 15. they'll;
16. you're; 17. aren't;
18. couldn't

Page 44

1. dog; 2. blow; 3. cup;
4. son; 5. flower;
6. number; 7. kick; 8. hour

Page 45

1. climb; 2. least; 3. sour;
4. see; 5. brush; 6. sad;
7. full;
baseball

Page 46

1. water; 2. notes;
3. drove; 4. river; 5. tame;
6. month; 7. awake;
8. women;
Check logic. Order of words may vary. *Open* is to *shut* as *soft* is to *hard*.

Scholastic Teaching Resources